Medical English Dialogues:

Clear & Simple Medical English Vocabulary for ESL/EFL Learners

Jackie Bolen

www.eslspeaking.org

Table of Contents

About the Author: Jackie Bolen

I taught English in South Korea for 10 years to every level and type of student. I've taught every age from kindergarten kids to adults. Most of my time has centered around teaching at two universities: five years at a science and engineering school in Cheonan, and four years at a major university in Busan where I taught upper-level classes for students majoring in English. In my spare time, you can usually find me outside surfing, biking, hiking, or snowshoeing. I now live in Vancouver, Canada.

In case you were wondering what my academic qualifications are, I hold a Master of Arts in Psychology. During my time in Korea, I completed both the Cambridge CELTA and DELTA certification programs. With the combination of almost ten years teaching ESL/EFL learners of all ages and levels, and the more formal teaching qualifications I've obtained, I have a solid foundation on which to offer advice to English learners.

Please send me an email with any questions or feedback that you might have.

YouTube: www.youtube.com/c/jackiebolen

Pinterest: www.pinterest.com/eslspeaking

ESL Speaking: www.eslspeaking.org

Email: jb.business.online@gmail.com

You might also be interested in these books (by Jackie Bolen):

- Short Stories in English for Intermediate Learners

- Master English Collocations in 15 Minutes a Day

- IELTS Academic Vocabulary Builder

Introduction to Medical English Dialogues

Welcome to this book designed to help you expand your knowledge of medical English. My goal is to help you speak more fluently and understand more of what you hear.

Let's face it, English can be difficult to master, even for the best students. In this book, you'll find dialogues that are ideal for intermediate-level students.

The best way to learn new vocabulary is in context.

To get the most bang for your buck, be sure to do the following:

- Review frequently.

- Try to use some of the phrases and expressions in real life.

- Don't be nervous about making mistakes. That's how you'll get better at English!

- Consider studying with a friend so you can help each other stay motivated.

- Use a notebook and write down new words, idioms, expressions, etc. that you run across. Review frequently so that they stay fresh in your mind.

- Be sure to answer the questions at the end of each dialogue. I recommend trying to do this from memory. No peeking!

- I recommend doing one dialogue a day. This will be more beneficial than finishing the entire book in a week or two.

Good luck and I wish you well on your journey to becoming more proficient with medical English.

Prescribing Antibiotics

Sammy is getting a prescription from his doctor.

Doctor: Sammy, I'm going to give you a **prescription** for a **broad-spectrum** antibiotic. You should take it twice a day, for an entire week. That'll clear up your **infection.**

Sammy: Okay.

Doctor: Some people find that they get an **upset stomach** when taking this medicine so I recommend taking it with breakfast and then after dinner. It's very important to finish the entire week, even if you start to feel better. Do you have any questions?

Sammy: Yes, I don't have **insurance** for **medication**. Is there a **generic** of this?

Doctor: Yes, there is. Just be sure to ask the **pharmacist** about that. Oh, and come back if you don't start to feel better after five or six days.

Vocabulary

Prescription: Written instructions that a doctor gives to a patient so that he or she can get medicine from the pharmacist.

Broad-spectrum: General; not specific.

Infection: Bacteria that are multiplying out of control.

Upset stomach: Stomachache.

Insurance: A premium paid to obtain protection against a specific problem. In the case of health insurance, the company will pay all or a portion of medical expenses.

Medication: Medicine.

Generic: Not brand name.

Pharmacist: Someone who fills a prescription by giving medicine to patients.

Practice

1. I'm not sure about that, can you please check with the _____?

2. Here's your _____ for the cream.

3. You have a sinus _____.

4. I'm looking for the cheapest option since I don't have _____.

5. Please take this _____ 3 times a day.

6. I'm going to give you a _____ antibiotic that should do the job.

7. If you get an _____, be sure to take it with some juice or a snack.

8. There is a _____ version. Would you like that?

Answers

1. pharmacist

2. prescription

3. infection

4. insurance

5. medication

6. broad-spectrum

7. upset stomach

8. generic

A Broken Leg

Erin is getting some bad news from her doctor about her leg.

Doctor: Okay. Let me pull up the **x-ray**. Hmm...it looks you have a **hairline fracture** right here.

Erin: Oh no! What does that mean? It's broken?

Doctor: Yes, it's broken and you'll need a **cast** for at least a few weeks. The good news is that it's just a small break and it should heal well. You won't need **surgery** because the bones are not **out of alignment.**

Erin: Okay.

Doctor: All right. The nurse will get everything organized for the cast and I'll be back in a few minutes to do it. She'll also get you organized for **crutches** and explain how to take a shower and stuff like that with a cast on.

Erin: Sure. Thank you.

Vocabulary

X-ray: A picture of the bones.

Hairline fracture: A very small break in a bone that is almost not visible at first glance.

Cast: A hard bandage or device that prevents something from moving to allow a bone to heal.

Surgery: Fixing a part of the body, usually by cutting into it.

Out of alignment: Not in order; not in the correct position or place.

Crutches: 2 sticks that are designed to help someone walk if they have a broken leg, foot, or ankle.

Practice

1. Do you know how to correctly use _____?

2. It looks like your shoulder is _____. Let me see if I can pop it back into place.

3. I'm hoping to avoid _____ on my knee but I'm not sure it'll be possible.

4. Let me take a look at this _____.

5. You can come back in six weeks to get your _____ taken off.

6. I have some good news and bad news. Your leg is broken but it's just a _____.

Answers

1. crutches

2. out of alignment

3. surgery

4. x-ray

5. cast

6. hairline fracture

A Hernia

Ted is talking to his doctor about his hernia.

Doctor: Okay, the test results are back Ted. It looks like you have a **hernia.**

Ted: What exactly is that?

Doctor: Well, it's a gap in the **muscles** in your **stomach** so that the contents of your **stomach** are not where they should be.

Ted: So what's the fix?

Doctor: We'll have to schedule you for a **minor operation** to put the piece of **intestine** back into the right place. While it is relatively minor and you won't have to stay overnight at the hospital, you might be looking at a few weeks of **recovery time.**

Ted: Okay, that sounds fine.

Vocabulary

Hernia: A gap in the muscles that allow the contents of the abdomen to poke through.

Muscles: Tissue in the body that holds the skeleton up and contracts to allow for movement.

Stomach: One part of the body that processes food.

Minor operation: A small surgery.

Intestine: The lower part of the digestive system.

Recovery time: How long it will take someone to get better after an injury or illness.

Practice

1. Your _____ will be 3-4 weeks.

2. Do you have a _____? I've heard that they can be very painful.

3. I wish I had a flatter _____.

4. Humans have a small _____ and a large _____.

5. How did he get such big _____? He must be working out all the time.

6. Don't worry. It's a _____ that we do all the time here.

Answers

1. recovery time

2. hernia

3. stomach

4. intestine

5. muscles

6. minor operation

Prescription Refill

Tess is calling to get a prescription refill from her doctor.

Tess: Hi, I'd like to get a **refill** on my prescription, please.

Receptionist: Okay. What's your name?

Tess: Tess Brown.

Receptionist: Sure, let me check. It's for the **birth control pills**?

Tess: Yes.

Receptionist: Unfortunately, we don't do refills for anything related to **birth control** over the phone. You'll have to make an appointment with your doctor.

Tess: Really? I got them refilled **over the phone** last time.

Receptionist: The government has recently changed their **policy** about this. Sorry about that.

Tess: Okay. I was thinking of getting an **IUD**. Does Dr. Jensen do this?

Receptionist: Yes, she does.

Vocabulary

Refill: To get more of something; to fill something up.

Birth control pills: Medicine that prevents unwanted pregnancy.

Birth control: Various methods to prevent unwanted pregnancy.

Over the phone: Using the telephone.

Policy: A course of action.

IUD: Intrauterine device. A small object that's inserted into the uterus to prevent pregnancy.

Vocabulary

1. Can I please get a _____ on this drink?

2. I'm trying to decide between an _____ and _____.

3. What's our company _____ on that?

4. Can I take care of this _____?

5. What method of _____ do you prefer?

Answers

1. refill

2. IUD/birth control pills

3. policy

4. over the phone

5. birth control

Talking about Recovery Time

Zeke is talking to his doctor about how long it will take to recover from his broken arm.

Zeke: Dr. Merk! How long until I get this **cast** off?

Dr. Merk: It'll be at least 8 weeks I'm afraid.

Zeke: Really? Why so long?

Dr. Merk: It's a serious **fracture.** We'll take the cast off and then **x-ray** it. You may need a cast longer than that, depending on the results.

Zeke: For real? And I can't drive at all?

Dr. Merk: I wouldn't recommend it. It can be quite dangerous if you can't bend your **elbow**.

Zeke: Okay.

Dr. Merk: And please keep in mind that even after you get the cast off, there will be some **recovery time**. You'll have to go to **physio** for at least a couple of months to regain strength and **muscle tone** in your arm.

Vocabulary

Cast: A hard shell or case for a broken bone.

Fracture: A break (usually refers to a bone).

X-ray: A machine that takes a picture of bones.

Elbow: The joint between the wrist and shoulder.

Recovery time: How much time it takes to get better after an injury or illness.

Physio: Physiotherapy; rehabilitation.

Muscle tone: The amount of tension in a muscle at rest.

Practice

1. I lost all the _____ in my leg after I broke it and was in a wheelchair for 3 months.

2. Call 911. It looks like an open _____.

3. It hurts a lot when you bump your _____.

4. I need to make a _____ appointment for my sore finger.

5. Come back in 6 weeks to get your _____ off.

6. Let's have a look at this _____.

7. How much _____ am I looking at?

Answers

1. muscle tone

2. fracture

3. elbow

4. physio

5. cast

6. x-ray

7. recovery time

Talking About Lifestyle Changes

Allen is talking to his doctor about some bad test results.

Allen: So what's the news doc?

Dr. Qi: Well, it's bad news. The results show **high cholesterol** and that you're **pre-diabetic**.

Allen: Oh no. Is there some medication for that?

Dr. Qi: Yes, but let's talk about your lifestyle first. Do you **smoke** or **drink**?

Allen: Yes, **a pack a day** usually. And I have **a 6-pack** every night usually.

Dr. Qi: And what about exercise?

Allen: What's that? Hahaha!

Dr. Qi: And finally, how about your **diet**?

Allen: Well, bacon is my favourite food and I don't like vegetables that much.

Dr. Qi: Okay. Well, that explains the high cholesterol. Let's talk about some **lifestyle changes** in those areas before getting you on medication.

Vocabulary

High cholesterol: A type of fat found in the blood that comes from eating animal products.

Pre-diabetic: Blood sugar levels are higher than they should be.

Smoke: Use cigarettes (a verb in this case)

Drink: Consume alcohol (a verb in this case).

A pack a day: Smoking an entire package of cigarettes every day.

A 6-pack: 6 cans of beer that are sold together in a package.

Diet: Food you eat.

Lifestyle changes: Making changes regarding smoking, drinking, sleeping, diet, etc.

Practice

1. You'll need to make some _____ if you want to avoid type 2 diabetes.

2. I had _____ so I adopted a vegan diet.

3. Wow! Ted likes to _____.

4. Let's pick up _____ for the party tonight.

5. If you _____, you have a higher chance of getting lung cancer.

6. What's your _____ like? Do you eat a lot of fruits and vegetables?

7. I'm _____ so am drastically changing my diet.

8. My brother smokes _____. I'm so worried about him.

Answers

1. lifestyle changes

2. high cholesterol

3. drink

4. a 6-pack

5. smoke

6. diet

7. pre-diabetic

8. a pack a day

A Physical Exam

Keith is getting an exam done by his doctor.

Doctor: When was the last time you came in for an exam?

Keith: I'm not sure. It's been a long time. Maybe two years.

Doctor: Okay, any problems that I should be aware of? Have you been feeling good?

Keith: No problems and I've been feeling pretty good, even though I just turned 50! I am taking **anti-depressants** though.

Doctor: I see. How's your mood now?

Keith: Much better since I started taking the medication.

Doctor: Okay, please **roll up your sleeve**. I'll take your **blood pressure**. That's good: **125/80**. And what about exercise? How often do you do it? And your diet?

Keith: Almost every day. I like to run and bike. I eat mostly **vegan** meals.

Doctor: I'm going to listen to your heart now. Okay. That sounds fine. I'm going to send you for a blood test to check your **cholesterol** and a few other things.

Vocabulary

Anti-depressants: Medicine designed to help people who are depressed.

Roll up your sleeve: What you need to do if you're getting a needle in your arm for a blood test, or getting your blood pressure taken. It means to lift (roll) up the arm on your shirt.

Blood pressure: How much pressure your heart exerts pumping blood over the force your heart exerts in between beats.

125/80 (one twenty five over eighty): Systolic pressure of the heart (when it pumps or beats) over diastolic pressure (the force at rest).

Vegan: Describes someone who doesn't consume animal products. Vegan meals are ones made without animal products.

Cholesterol: The amount of fat in the blood. Cholesterol comes from consuming meat and dairy products.

Practice

1. No thanks. I can't eat ice cream these days. My doctor said that my _____ is way too high.

2. Please _____ now. This will hurt a little bit.

3. I'm trying to make more _____ meals for my family but my teenage boys have been resisting me.

4. Your _____ is excellent for someone in their 80's.

5. Have you had your blood pressure checked lately? Oh, I think it's around _____.

6. I'm going to give you a prescription for some _____ and recommend a counsellor.

Answers

1. cholesterol

2. roll up your sleeve

3. vegan

4. blood pressure

5. 125/80

6. anti-depressants

Talking about Insurance Coverage

Sid and the receptionist are talking about Sid's insurance.

Receptionist: Do you have **insurance coverage**?

Sid: Yes, Pacific Blue Cross. Here's my card.

Receptionist: Okay, I'll enter your information into the system. We can **bill them directly**.

Sid: Perfect. How much will be **covered** today?

Receptionist: Let me check and see what it comes back with.

Sid: Okay.

Receptionist: It looks like they'll cover 80% of your **procedure**. So you'll have to pay around $300 **out of pocket** but it could be up to $500. It depends on what the **surgeon** finds. Is that okay with you?

Sid: Yes, that's fine.

Vocabulary

Insurance coverage: An active policy with an insurance company. In this case, to cover medical expenses.

Bill them directly: The doctor, dentist, physiotherapist, etc. gets money from the insurance company instead of the patient for medical services.

Covered: Paid for.

Procedure: Less serious medical operation.

Out of pocket: The portion of the bill that the insurance company doesn't pay.

Surgeon: A doctor who performs operations.

Practice

1. You'll have to ask your _____ about that. I'm not sure.

2. My _____ is useless—it covers nothing.

3. What percentage is _____?

4. I'll have the _____ on Tuesday at 10:00.

5. Can you _____ for that?

6. You'll have to pay around $500 _____ for the operation.

Answers

1. surgeon

2. insurance coverage

3. covered

4. procedure

5. bill them directly

6. out of pocket

Making an Appointment

Tom is making an appointment to see his doctor.

Tom: Can I make an appointment for tomorrow, please?

Receptionist: Sure, with which doctor?

Tom: Dr. Brown.

Receptionist: Have you been here before?

Tom: Yes, my name is Tom Watson.

Receptionist: We have nothing tomorrow but how about Wednesday?

Tom: Sure, that's fine.

Receptionist: Is 2:00 okay?

Tom: Yes, that's okay.

Receptionist: What are you coming in for?

Tom: A sore toe.

Receptionist: All right, we'll see you then.

Check your Understanding

1. When's Tom's appointment?

2. Does he have a serious problem?

3. Who is Tom's Doctor?

4. Is Wednesday his first choice for appointment?

Answers

1. His appointment is on Wednesday at 2:00.

2. No, he has a sore toe.

3. His doctor is Dr. Brown.

4. No, it's not.

Rescheduling an Appointment

Tom needs to reschedule his doctor's appointment

Tom: Hi, this is Tom Watson. I have an appointment with Dr. Brown on Wednesday at 2:00 but I won't be able to make it.

Receptionist: Let me look it up. Okay, got it. Do you need to reschedule?

Tom: Yes, please. Do you have anything for Thursday or Friday?

Receptionist: Yes, how about Thursday at 2:30?

Tom: I'll take it. Thank you.

Receptionist: Okay, see you Thursday at 2:30.

Check your Understanding

1. Do we know why Tom had to cancel his appointment?

2. When was his original appointment?

3. When's his new appointment?

Answers

1. No, we don't.

2. On Wednesday at 2:00.

3. On Thursday at 2:30.

Urgent Appointment Request

Andy is calling his doctor trying to get an urgent appointment.

Receptionist: Hi, Dr. Lee's office.

Andy: Hi, yes. Do you have any appointments today? It's quite **urgent**.

Receptionist: What's the problem?

Andy: I'm having trouble breathing. I can't take a deep breath. I have **asthma** but it's never been this bad. And my **heart is racing**.

Receptionist: It sounds like you should go to the ER. Or, even call **911**. Breathing difficulties are very serious. We don't have the **specialized equipment** to help with that stuff at our office.

Andy: Okay. I'll go to the ER right now.

Receptionist: Do you have an **inhaler** for asthma? Please use that and take it with you.

Andy: Yes, I have it with me right now.

Vocabulary

Urgent: Describes something that requires immediate attention.

Asthma: A lung condition that sometimes makes breathing difficult.

Heart is racing: The heart is beating faster than it should (or at least it feels like that to the person).

911: In many countries, the number you dial to call an ambulance to your location.

Specialized equipment: Specific machines to deal with a certain situation.

Inhaler: A device that disperses medicine into the lungs in aerosol form (most often used by people with asthma).

Practice

1. You'll need to go to VGH for any eye problems. They have the _____ there.

2. I have _____ so need to be careful about not going on hikes that are too difficult.

3. Call _____ right now. I think I'm having a heart attack.

4. I don't think I can wait until tomorrow. It's _____.

5. Don't forget your _____ Timmy.

6. My _____. I'm so nervous about this interview.

Answers

1. specialized equipment

2. asthma

3. 911

4. urgent

5. inhaler

6. heart is racing

Test Results

Jess and her doctor are discussing some test results.

Doctor: How are you feeling today? A bit better I hope?

Jess: Yes, definitely. I haven't felt **nauseous** since I switched the medication.

Doctor: Okay good. I have your test results here.

Jess: Is it good news or bad news?

Doctor: Well, a bit of both. You'll need **surgery** to remove the **tumour** in your leg. However, the **biopsy** showed that it's **benign**.

Jess: Benign? Isn't that bad?

Doctor: Oh no. Sorry for using **doctor jargon**. It's not **cancerous**. But we should remove it because it's getting bigger and will soon make it more difficult for you to play soccer and do other stuff like that.

Jess: Okay. That's good news then. When can I get the surgery?

Doctor: Please talk to the receptionist after our appointment. She'll give the **surgeon** a call and get you all set up. It's usually a 2-3 month wait for less urgent situations like yours.

Jess: Okay. Thank you.

Vocabulary

Nauseous: Feeling sick to your stomach, like you might throw up (vomit).

Surgery: A procedure on the body, usually involves cutting under the skin, or into another part of the body (the eye for example).

Tumour: A mass or growth inside the body that shouldn't be there. Can be cancerous, or not.

Biopsy: Removing a small sample of tissue from inside the body to do tests on (usually for cancer).

Benign: Not cancerous or dangerous.

Doctor jargon: Words that doctors use which patients don't understand.

Cancerous: Describes something that has cancer cells.

Surgeon: A person who does surgery.

Practice

1. I need to book an appointment with the _____ but she's booked up for months because of Covid delays.

2. I just found out that I have a _____ in my stomach. I have to wait and see if it's cancerous, or not.

3. I'm so relieved. My doctor just let me know that my tumour is _____.

4. I have a lump on my arm. I hope it's not _____ but I'm scared to go to the doctor and find out.

5. I'm scheduled for _____ on May 29th and 7:00 in the morning. Can you take me?

6. I have to get a _____ on this tumour to find out if it's cancerous. I hope it isn't.

7. My son always gets _____ when riding in a car.

8. I want to switch doctors. Mine always uses _____ that I don't understand. I haven't been to medical school! It's weird that he doesn't understand this.

Answers

1. surgeon

2. tumour

3. benign

4. cancerous

5. surgery

6. biopsy

7. nauseous

8. doctor jargon

Talking about Extra Fees

Jen is talking to the receptionist about paying for her surgery.

Receptionist: Let's get your insurance and financial stuff all taken care of before the surgery.

Jen: Sure. Here's my **insurance card**.

Receptionist: Let me check what's **covered**. Okay, it looks like most of it won't be covered as your company considers this to be an **elective** procedure.

Jen: Oh really. So **how much am I looking at**?

Receptionist: All in, it should be about $3000, including however many **follow-up visits** you need. If there are any **complications** during surgery, it may be up to $5000.

Jen: Hmm. I didn't know this. I should have phoned my insurance company before this I guess.

Receptionist: Do you still want to go through with it?

Jen: No, I can't afford it.

Receptionist: Okay. Unfortunately, we charge a $500 **cancellation fee** for less than 24 hours notice which this qualifies for. Sorry about that.

Vocabulary

Insurance card: A card that you can keep in your wallet with policy number, coverage dates, etc. for insurance.

Covered: Describes what the insurance company will pay for.

Elective: Optional.

How much am I looking at?: Asking about the final amount something will cost.

All in: In total.

Follow-up visits: A subsequent visit with the doctor after the surgery or procedure to make sure everything is going well.

Complications: Things that may go wrong; the unexpected.

Cancellation fee: How much is charged if you cancel an appointment without appropriate notice (depends on the specific policy for the company/doctor).

Practice

1. What's the _____ for less than 24 hours?

2. I'm not sure I can afford that. _____?

3. Do you have your _____ with you? I'll need the group number and the policy number.

4. Most people need 2-3 _____ after this procedure so we'll schedule those now as well. You can cancel them if you don't need them.

5. There are certainly some _____ that can happen with this surgery. I'll explain the most common ones to you.

6. This surgery is _____ and we don't cover it, unfortunately.

7. How much of the cleaning and check-up is _____ by my insurance?

8. It's going to be $1000 _____. I think it's reasonable.

Answers

1. cancellation fee

2. How much am I looking at?

3. insurance card

4. follow-up visits

5. complications

6. elective

7. covered

8. all-in

Talking about Pain

Sam is talking to his doctor about his stomach pain.

Doctor: What brings you in today?

Sam: Well, I've been having lots of **stomach** pain. Sometimes it hurts after I eat, but sometimes it doesn't. It's been happening for about 6 months now.

Doctor: Have you changed your **eating habits** lately?

Sam: Not really. I've stopped eating so often because I don't want my stomach to hurt.

Doctor: What's the pain level, on a **scale of 1 to 10**? And any other areas?

Sam: Not terrible. Maybe only a 2 or 3. And just in my stomach.

Doctor: Okay, can you lay down on the **exam table**? I want to press on areas of your stomach to see what I can find. Hmm. It doesn't hurt when I press any of these areas?

Sam: No, not really.

Doctor: Okay. We'll need to run some tests then. I'm going to do a **blood test** for all the major things and why don't we schedule you for an **ultrasound** as well?

Vocabulary

Stomach: The part of the body that processes food.

Eating habits: A general way to describe what and how someone eats.

Scale of 1 to 10: A way to describe pain. 1 is nothing and 10 is the worst pain.

Exam table: A table in a doctor's office where patients can be examined.

Blood test: Taking blood from a patient using a needle to look for various factors.

Ultrasound: A test that looks at internal structures or organs in the body.

Practice

1. Why don't I schedule you for an _____? I think we'll know a lot more after that.

2. How much does it hurt on a _____?

3. I ate so much at the buffet that my _____ looks bigger!

4. It's a simple _____ to find out if you're pregnant, or not.

5. Can you please sit on the _____? I want to take a look at that knee of yours.

6. Have you changed your _____ lately? Maybe more fatty foods?

Answers

1. ultrasound

2. scale of 1 to 10

3. stomach

4. blood test

5. exam table

6. eating habits

Talking about Joint Pain

Sid is talking to his doctor about some pain that he's having.

Doctor: What brings you in today?

Sid: Well, I've been having lots of pain in my knees lately.

Doctor: Both knees or just one? And any other **joints**?

Sid: Both knees but no other joints.

Doctor: Is there a particular time that it hurts?

Sid: They **ache** most of the time but are especially bad after going for a walk or when the weather starts to change. And they're very **stiff** in the morning but it gets better throughout the day.

Doctor: Have you had any previous issues with them or been **diagnosed** with anything?

Sid: No, this is the first time in my life that I've had issues with my knees.

Doctor: Okay, please lay down on the **exam table**. I'm going to check for **swelling** and **range of motion.**

Sid: Sure.

Doctor: I suspect you may be in the beginning stages of **arthritis**. I'm going to send you for an **ultrasound** and an **x-ray** to see what's going on in there.

Vocabulary

Joints: The connection between parts of the body. For example, ankles, knees, elbows, etc.

Ache: Pain that isn't extreme but is present for a long time.

Stiff: Not flexible or limber.

Diagnosed: Identified with a specific problem.

Exam table: The table in a doctor's office where people sit or lay down.

Swelling: When a part of the body is bigger than normal, often due to fluid build-up.

Range of motion: The full movement possible for a joint.

Arthritis: Inflammation or swelling of the joints.

Ultrasound: A type of medical imaging that is used to see inside the body.

X-ray: A type of medical imaging that looks at bones.

Practice

1. Let's get an _____ of your hand to see if it's broken.

2. I usually feel pretty _____ the day after going hiking.

3. I'm going for my first _____ today! I'm so excited to meet my new baby.

4. My _____ are shot from playing basketball for so many years when I was young.

5. Can you please sit down on the _____?

6. Since you have joint pain in your knees and elbows, I suspect you could have _____.

7. I've been _____ with a tumour in my stomach. They took a biopsy.

8. I have an _____ in my bones that won't go away.

9. I'd like to check your _____ in your shoulder.

10. It looks like you have some _____ in your knee. Did you do lots of exercise lately?

Answers

1. x-ray

2. stiff

3. ultrasound

4. joints

5. exam table

6. arthritis

7. diagnosed

8. ache

9. range of motion

10. swelling

Talking about Recovery Time

Anne is talking to her doctor about how long her recovery time will be.

Anne: So how much longer before I can play tennis?

Doctor: Well, you had quite a serious **wrist sprain**. It'll be at least four weeks and could be closer to six or eight. Have you booked a **physio** appointment?

Anne: No, do I need to?

Doctor: Yes, for sprains, I always recommend physio. They will **cut down** your **recovery time** and you'll be back to the tennis courts a lot sooner.

Anne: Okay, I'll do that. Should I wear a wrist **brace**?

Doctor: That's maybe not necessary. Just be very careful with it when you're going about your **daily activities**. Some people find that wearing one at night can be helpful, especially if they move around a lot in the night and wake up with a sore wrist.

Anne: Okay. Sounds good. Do I need to make a follow-up appointment?

Doctor: No, you should be back to normal in a month or so with physio. But, if it's not improving, then come back and see me.

Vocabulary

Wrist: The connecting joint between the hand and the arm.

Sprain: Harm to a joint but not as serious as a break.

Physio: Physiotherapy.

Cut down: Reduce

Recovery time: How long it takes to get better.

Brace: A device designed to add support or restrict movement.

Practice

1. I have a serious ankle _____ so won't be able to play basketball for a few months at least.

2. I have to _____ on my smoking to improve my overall health.

3. Have you considered getting an ankle _____? It might prevent all these sprains you keep getting.

4. I'm going to make a _____ appointment this week.

5. Be careful with your _____ when you work with the computer all day.

6. The _____ shouldn't be too long—maybe only 1-2 weeks.

Answers

1. sprain

2. cut down

3. brace

4. physio

5. wrist

6. recovery time

Finding a Family Doctor

Receptionist: Hi, Dr. Brown and Dr. Park's office.

Lindsey: Hi there, I'm wondering if you have any doctors who are accepting new **patients**?

Receptionist: Yes, Dr. Park is accepting new patients in her **family practice**.

Lindsey: Oh, okay. What's the process?

Receptionist: You can make a 30-minute "**meet and greet**" appointment to chat with her and see if it's **a good fit** for both of you.

Lindsey: Can I do that?

Receptionist: Yes, for just you or other family members?

Lindsey: For myself and my two kids. They are 10 and 14.

Receptionist: Okay. How about Thursday at 1:00? Your kids don't have to come, just you.

Lindsey: Sure, that sounds good. Do I have to do anything with my previous **medical records**?

Receptionist: Not yet. We can take care of that **in person**.

Vocabulary

Patients: People who are under the care of a medical professional.

Family practice: Describes a doctor who looks after all general problems for patients and is easily accessible.

Meet and greet: An informal chat to get to know someone.

Medical records: Details about a person's previous treatment, medications, etc. from a doctor.

In person: In real life, not over the Internet or phone.

Practice

1. I much prefer _____ classes compared to ones over Zoom.

2. My friend is opening a _____. Why don't you call and see if he'll be your doctor?

3. Let's organize a _____ for the new donors.

4. On average, I see 4 _____ an hour.

5. Can you please request your _____ to be sent over here from your old doctor?

Answers

1. in person

2. family practice

3. meet and greet

4. patients

5. medical records

You have Cancer

Sarah is getting some bad news from her doctor.

Doctor: Hi Sarah, I'm afraid that I have some bad news for you. The tests that we did show that you have **liver cancer**. I'm so sorry.

Sarah: Ohhh. How serious is it?

Doctor: Well, it's spread to some of your other **organs** now too so the **survival rate** for this kind of thing is very low. You may only have a few more months to live.

Sarah: Is there treatment for it?

Doctor: Yes, **chemotherapy** and **radiation** are possibilities and they may extend your life by a few months but a cure is very unlikely. They do have a lot of **side effects** and may reduce the **quality of life** that you do have left. Most people in your situation ultimately decide on treatment that will just make their last few months more comfortable.

Sarah: Okay. Let me think about it and do some more research. Can I call you if I have questions?

Doctor: Of course, why don't you make an appointment for early next week and we can talk about what you've decided. Why don't I call you in a couple of days as well and see if you have any questions?

Sarah: Okay. Thank you.

Vocabulary

Liver: An organ in the body.

Cancer: A disease where abnormal cells multiply rapidly in the body.

Organs: A part of the body that is self-contained and has a specific function. For example, the heart which pumps blood, or the lungs which exchange carbon dioxide and oxygen.

Survival rate: What percentage of people are still living after a certain length of time after diagnosis.

Chemotherapy: A treatment for cancer that involves using drugs to kill cancer cells.

Radiation: A treatment for cancer that uses radiation to kill cancer cells.

Side effects: A secondary, undesirable effect of something.

Quality of life: The standard of health or comfort experienced by a person or group of people.

Practice

1. My _____ improved so much when I moved and could walk to work.

2. I'm sorry to tell you that you have lung _____.

3. We've found that radiation doesn't work as well as _____ for this type of cancer.

4. There will be lots of _____ from this medication, including nausea and fatigue.

5. The _____ is the part of the body that can get easily damaged by too much alcohol.

6. The _____ for this type of cancer is only 2% after 5 years.

7. _____ is the best option for your type of cancer but it does have a lot of side effects.

8. The hearts, kidneys and lungs are examples of _____.

Answers

1. quality of life

2. cancer

3. chemotherapy

4. side effects

5. liver

6. survival rate

7. radiation

8. organs

Getting a Doctor's Note

Kim is asking her doctor for a note to excuse her from work.

Kim: Is it possible to get a note from you to excuse me from work?

Doctor: Yes, but there's a fee for that service. Please talk to the receptionist.

Kim: Okay.

Kim: Hi, could I please get a note to excuse me from work?

Receptionist: Definitely. We do charge $20 for that. Is that okay?

Kim: Sure, no problem.

Receptionist: Okay, give me a couple of minutes to get that done for you. Have a seat and I'll call you up.

Kim: Great. Thank you.

Check your Understanding

1. Is the note free?

2. Who is going to prepare the note?

3. Why does Kim need a doctor's note?

Answers

1. No, it costs $20.

2. The receptionist will do it.

3. She needs a note to excuse her from work.

Throwing Up

Jen is talking to her doctor about throwing up.

Doctor: What brings you here today?

Jen: I'm been throwing up.

Doctor: How long have you been **vomiting**?

Jen: For about 2 days now. I thought it was going to stop but it didn't.

Doctor: Have you had any **diarrhea**?

Jen: No.

Doctor: Okay, I'm going to feel your stomach and listen to your heart. No problems there.

Did you eat anything unusual in the day or two before you started throwing up?

Jen: Hmmm. Let me think. Oh, I did go out to a new Italian place and had some seafood.

Doctor: You may have **food poisoning**. Or, it could be the **stomach flu**. Either way, I'll give you some **antibiotics** and you should feel better soon. Plus I'll give you **a shot** to calm your stomach down. Drink lots of **fluids**. If you don't feel better in 48 hours, come see me.

Vocabulary

Vomiting: Throwing up.

Diarrhea: A bowel movement that is forceful and watery.

Food poisoning: A sickness that is caused by eating food that is bad/rotten.

Stomach flu: A sickness with nausea, diarrhea, vomiting, or cramps.

Antibiotics: Medicine that kills bacteria.

A shot: Medicine that is given with a needle.

Fluids: Liquid things.

Practice

1. Do I have to get _____? I'm so scared of needles.

2. Have you been _____? You might be dehydrated.

3. I'm going to give you a prescription for some _____. That should clear things up quickly for you.

4. I'm sure I got _____ from eating those mussels the other day.

5. If you have the _____, please don't come to school! It's very contagious.

6. Drink lots of _____ on a hot day to avoid heatstroke.

7. Dude! Too much information. I didn't need to know that you have _____.

Answers

1. a shot

2. vomiting

3. antibiotics

4. food poisoning

5. stomach flu

6. fluids

7. diarrhea

At the Pharmacy

Keith is at the pharmacy to get his prescription refilled.

Keith: Hi, I have this **prescription** to **drop off.**

Pharmacist: Sure, no problem. I can get that ready for you. It'll be about a 20-minute wait.

Keith: Sure, I'll be here.

Pharmacist: Keith? I have your prescription. Have you taken this **medication** before?

Keith: No, I haven't.

Pharmacist: Okay. You should take it 3 times a day, with meals. These **antibiotics** can give you an **upset stomach** which is why you should take them with food.

Keith: Sure.

Pharmacist: They also have some side effects besides the upset stomach. You might feel very thirsty, have a headache or feel **fatigued**. See your doctor if they are **bothering** you. One last thing. Be sure to finish the entire prescription, even if you start to feel better. It's important for killing all the bacteria.

Vocabulary

Prescription: An authorization for medication or treatment from a doctor.

Drop off: Leave something.

Medication: Medicine.

Antibiotics: Medicine that kills bacteria.

Upset stomach: Nausea, cramps or vomiting.

Fatigued: Tired.

Bothering: Annoying.

Practice

1. Sorry for _____ you with another question.

2. I'd like to _____ my car and pick it up in a couple of hours when you're done. Will that work?

3. You'll need to take these _____ for 10 days.

4. If you're feeling _____, try getting more sleep.

5. I'm going to give you a _____ for some cream that should clear up your rash.

6. Have you taken any over-the-counter _____ for it?

7. Try drinking some ginger tea if you have an _____.

Answers

1. bothering

2. drop off

3. antibiotics

4. fatigued

5. prescription

6. medication

7. upset stomach

Athlete's Foot

Ted is talking to the pharmacist about his rash.

Ted: Hi, excuse me. I'm wondering if you can recommend something for the **rash** on my feet?

Pharmacist: What seems to be the problem.

Ted: Well, they are kind of **itchy** and **stinky**, even after I take a shower. They also are super dry.

Pharmacist: Hmmm...sounds kind of like **athlete's foot.** You'd have to see your doctor to be sure but you could try out some of this **anti-fungal cream**.

Ted: Okay, I'll give it a try.

Pharmacist: And **fungus** loves moist and hot so be sure to take a shower right after exercising. Use foot powder too to keep things dry in there.

Ted: Sure thing. I'll give it a try. Thank you.

Pharmacist: You're welcome.

Vocabulary

Rash: Irritated or swollen skin.

Itchy: Describes a part of the body that you want to itch or rub because it feels irritated.

Stinky: Smelling bad.

Athlete's foot: Fungal infection that is commonly found on the feet, especially between the toes.

Anti-fungal cream: A cream designed to kill fungus.

Fungus: A spore-producing organism.

Practice

1. Wow! It looks like some kind of _____ has gone crazy in your compost.

2. My arm, under my cast, is so _____.

3. Try out this _____ for your feet.

4. Babies often get a _____ because of diapers.

5. You for sure have _____. Take care of that!

6. I get so _____ when I exercise.

Answers

1. fungus

2. itchy

3. anti-fungal cream

4. rash

5. athlete's foot

6. stinky

Under the Weather

Jerry is talking to Linda about how he doesn't feel well.

Linda: How are you doing these days Jerry?

Jerry: Oh, not great. I'm always sick it seems like.

Linda: I've told you so many times to take better care of your health!

Jerry: I know, I know. My mom used to tell me to not be such a **couch potato** and that **an apple a day keeps the doctor away**. I wish that I'd listened to her! I'm feeling **worse for wear.**

Linda: Keep your chin up! I know you're **feeling under the weather** but **this too shall pass.**

Jerry: Thanks Linda, I appreciate you **checking in on** me every day.

Linda: It's the least I can do. You've helped me with so many things over the years. Just don't **kick the bucket** on me, okay?

Vocabulary

Feeling under the weather: Not feeling well; feeling sick.

Keep your chin up: Telling someone to stay strong. Encouraging someone in a tough situation.

Couch potato: Someone who spends lots of time on the couch watching TV or movies or playing video games. Not active.

An apple a day keeps the doctor away: Eating healthy keeps you from getting sick.

This too shall pass: A bad time that will eventually end.

Checking in on: To see how someone is doing.

It's the least I can do: No problem; it's a small thing, usually when you feel like you should do more.

Worse for wear: Feeling worn out or tired.

Kick the bucket: Die.

Practice

1. My dad keeps phoning and _____ me. It's almost too much!

2. I keep nagging my son to get active because he's such a _____.

3. I called in sick because I was feeling a bit _____.

4. My mom is great at telling people to _____ when something bad happens.

5. I'm convinced that the saying, "_____" really does work!

6. My son has been pretty down lately but I told him that, "_____."

7. Lunch is on me. _____, seeing as you've been making my meals all week.

8. I'm _____ after being in the hospital for more than a week. It was impossible to sleep there.

9. I hope that I don't _____ before I'm 80 but I'm nervous about how much I smoke!

Answers

1. checking in on

2. couch potato

3. under the weather

4. keep your chin up

5. An apple a day keeps the doctor away

6. This too shall pass

7. It's the least I can do

8. worse for wear

9. kick the bucket

Over-the-Counter Medications

Ted and Anita are talking about going to the doctor.

Ted: Hey Anita, what's up?

Anita: I've had a rough couple of weeks. I **caught a cold** and it took me a while to recover. I was just **getting ready** for Christmas too. It was **terrible timing**.

Ted: Oh no! Did you **go to the doctor**?

Anita: Yes, she said to take some **over-the-counter medications** because it was a virus.

Ted: Well, that's better than **taking antibiotics** when you don't need to. I think that happens **quite often** but it's certainly not a good thing.

Anita: Enough about me. How are you?

Ted: Well, I **had the flu** last month and I'm just **fully recovered** now.

Vocabulary

Caught a cold: Got sick with a cold.

Getting ready: Preparing.

Terrible timing: A bad time for something negative to happen.

Go to the doctor: See the doctor for an appointment.

Over-the-counter medications: Medicine that doesn't require a prescription.

Taking antibiotics: Taking medicine that kills harmful bacteria.

Quite often: Happens frequently.

Enough about me: I've been talking too much about myself!

Had the flu: Was sick with the flu but okay now.

Fully recovered: Not sick anymore.

Practice

1. I was sick for almost a month but I'm now _____.

2. Please _____. You're sick!

3. My son _____ from the other kids at school.

4. I _____ for almost two months. It was terrible.

5. Well, _____. What's happening with you these days?

6. He is _____ late for work.

7. That's _____ for getting sick. November is your busiest month at work, right?

8. I've been _____ for my ear infection but it's not getting better.

9. I'm well stocked with _____ at home.

10. _____ for work takes me at least an hour.

Answers

1. fully recovered

2. go to the doctor

3. caught a cold

4. had the flu

5. enough about me

6. quite often

7. terrible timing

8. taking antibiotics

9. over-the-counter medications

10. Getting ready

A Rash on My Arm

Jenny is talking to her doctor about a rash on her arm.

Doctor: Hi Jenny, what brings you here today?

Jenny: I have this strange **rash** on my arm.

Doctor: How long have you had it?

Jenny: For 6 months now.

Doctor: Do you have it on other parts of your body?

Jenny: No, just my left arm.

Doctor: Okay, is it **itchy**?

Jenny: Mostly at night.

Doctor: Is there anything that makes it better or worse?

Jenny: I've tried some **cortisone cream** and different **moisturizers** but it's still the same.

Doctor: I'm going to **prescribe** this **cream**. It works well for most rashes. Let's see if that clears it up. Come back in a month if that doesn't work. Oh, and one more thing. Take shorter showers that aren't so hot. A lot of people get rashes like this because their skin is too dry.

Vocabulary

Rash: Irritated or swollen skin.

Itchy: A part of the skin that you want to rub because it's irritated.

Cortisone cream: A cream that can reduce inflammation or allergic reactions.

Moisturizers: Something designed to add or retain moisture in the skin.

Prescribe: What a doctor does when they recommend medication to a patient.

Cream: Ointment.

Practice

1. Do you have any _____ for this rash? I'm not sure what to try.

2. My son has a _____ on his legs. It's maybe poison ivy I think.

3. I've tried lots of different _____ but my hands are still so dry.

4. My secret for mosquito bites is to use _____ on them.

5. I'm going to _____ an antibiotic for you.

6. It's usually quite _____ at night.

Answers

1. cream

2. rash

3. moisturizers

4. cortisone cream

5. prescribe

6. itchy

Intensive Care

Jerry and Linda are talking about Jerry's dad who was just in the hospital.

Jerry: To **add insult to injury**, my dad got Covid-19 when he was in the hospital for a heart attack.

Linda: Oh no. Is he okay?

Jerry: Well, he's not **out of the woods** yet. He's still **sick as a dog** but he's not **at death's door**. They just moved him from **intensive care** to the Covid-19 ward.

Linda: Is he still sick from Covid-19 or the heart attack?

Jerry: A bit of A, a bit of B. He was in poor health even before the heart attack.

Linda: Send him my **best wishes**, okay?

Jerry: Don't waste your breath. He still acts like he got up on the **wrong side of the bed** all the time.

Linda: Well, you certainly don't **take after** him. Don't worry!

Vocabulary

Add insult to Injury: Make something already bad worse. For example, a guy fell off his bike but then a car ran over his foot.

Out of the woods: A difficult situation that has improved. Usually refers to medical things when someone is very sick but has recovered a little bit.

Don't waste your breath: Whatever you say doesn't make a difference.

Sick as a dog: Very unwell.

At death's door: Close to dying.

Intensive care: The place in a hospital where you can find critically sick people.

Wrong side of the bed: Grumpy.

Best wishes: Friendly hope that someone is doing well.

Take after: Usually a son/daughter who is similar to his/her mother/father.

59

Practice

1. My sister hates mornings and often gets up on the _____.

2. My sister just got moved to _____. She got worse overnight.

3. I was _____ last year and spent a week in the hospital.

4. He's doing better but he's not _____ yet.

5. I can't believe he made it! He was _____.

6. _____. I've already made up my mind.

7. I honestly don't want to _____ but it looks like you have a flat tire too.

8. _____ on your recent engagement!

9. I hope my son doesn't _____ me. I haven't been the best example for him growing up.

Answers

1. wrong side of the bed

2. intensive care

3. sick as a dog

4. out of the woods

5. at death's door

6. Don't waste your breath

7. add insult to injury

8. Best wishes

9. take after

Going to the ER

Sam and Kerry are talking about an accident.

Sam: Oh Kerry! What happened?

Kerry: I hit a rock while riding my bike and went over the handlebars.

Sam: Oh no! It looks bad.

Kerry: I had to go to the ER. I hit my head pretty hard but no serious damage because I was wearing a helmet. Just a cut on my leg and some scrapes on my hands.

Sam: Thank god for that. How did you not break any bones?

Kerry: I'm not sure. It's a small miracle I think. They did an x-ray of my entire body to check and I also got a CAT scan of my head which was interesting. They were worried about bleeding in my brain.

Sam: I'm happy to hear that you're okay!

Check Your Understanding

1. How did Kerry get hurt?

2. Were Kerry's injuries serious?

3. Did the doctors think Kerry might have serious injuries?

Answers

1. He fell off his bike.

2. No, they weren't.

3. Yes, they did. They thought he might have bleeding in his brain.

Lots of Stomachaches

Carrie is discussing her problem with the doctor.

Doctor: Hi Carrie, what can I help you with today?

Carrie: I've been having lots of stomachaches lately.

Doctor: I see. Have you changed your diet recently?

Carrie: No, just the usual.

Doctor: What about stress? Any big thing coming up?

Carrie: Yes, I just changed jobs. I'm having trouble sleeping too.

Doctor: Do you think that might be the cause of it?

Carrie: It could be. It's been very stressful learning all the new systems at work.

Doctor: Are you exercising and eating healthy foods?

Carrie: No, I don't have time.

Doctor: That might make a big difference.

Check your Understanding

1. Does the doctor suggest medicine?

2. What is likely causing the stomachaches?

3. What other problem does she have besides stomachaches?

Answers

1. No, the doctor suggests exercise and eating healthy foods.

2. It might be stress from a new job.

3. She's also having trouble sleeping.

Whiplash

Joanna and Janice are talking about a recent accident.

Joanna: Hey, how are you doing? I heard that you got into a car accident recently.

Janice: Yes. I got rear-ended a couple of weeks ago.

Joanna: Was it serious?

Janice: Well, I didn't go to the hospital or even a walk-in clinic but I started to feel poorly later that night.

Joanna: What happened?

Janice: Even though there wasn't that much damage to my car, I did get whiplash. I'm still recovering and have to go to physio all the time. I had to take time off work too. My doctor thinks it'll still be a few months of recovery.

Joanna: That's tough for sure. Did you get some money from insurance for it?

Janice: Not yet. It's still too early for that. I have to recover from my injuries first before we settle. I may have to go to court as well.

Check Your Understanding

1. What bad thing happened to Janice?

2. When did the accident happen?

3. What injury did she get?

Answers

1. She got into a car accident.

2. It happened about two weeks ago.

3. She got whiplash.

Getting Stitches

Kay and Sid are talking about Sid's injuries from playing tennis.

Kay: So what did you get up to **this weekend** Sid? Wait...what happened to your face? That looks like it hurts.

Sid: I had a **tennis match** and I got hit in the face with the ball. It's just a **minor injury** but I had to go to the **emergency room** to **get stitches**. I couldn't get the bleeding to stop. It was quite a deep cut.

Kay: It doesn't look so minor! Good thing you didn't sustain **serious injuries**. It could have been bad if you'd gotten hit in the eye.

Sid: Yeah, nothing serious as long as I **take antibiotics** to **prevent infection**. I may have a scar on my face too. The worst thing was that we lost the match because I had to leave to go to the hospital.

Vocabulary

This weekend: Previous, or next Saturday or Sunday (depends on when talking about it— earlier, or later in the week).

Tennis match: Tennis game that consists of 3 or 5 sets.

Minor injury: Not a serious injury.

Emergency room: Place to get immediate medical treatment.

Get stitches: Using a needle and thread to close a cut in the skin.

Serious injuries: A big medical problem.

Take antibiotics: Taking pills to stop the spread of infection.

Prevent infection: Taking antibiotics or cleaning a wound so that bacteria don't get out of control.

Practice

1. Do you want to catch a movie with me _____?

2. Clean the wound first to help _____.

3. Did you have to _____ for that cut?

4. It looks worse than it is. It's just a _____.

5. Did you see the _____ between Nadal and Federer?

6. You'll have to _____ for that but please finish them all.

7. Please call 911 for _____.

8. I think I need to go to the _____. My arm is probably broken.

Answers

1. this weekend

2. prevent infection

3. get stitches

4. minor injury

5. tennis match

6. take antibiotics

7. serious injuries

8. emergency room

The First Aid Course

Ken and Tim are talking about a first aid course.

Ken: So what are you doing this weekend?

Tim: Oh, I'm taking a **first aid** course. You never know when I might have to **save someone's life**.

Ken: Wow! You go to **great lengths** to **do good** in this world.

Tim: Oh, I just like to **do the right thing**. Plus, I like to **stay busy** and fill up my **free time** with interesting things.

Ken: Well, **break a leg**. I'm sure it'll be useful working with kids. They're always injuring themselves. Did you know that I did an industrial first aid course years ago? My company paid for it so I volunteered.

Tim: Oh, interesting! I'll call you if I have any questions.

Vocabulary

First aid: Basic medical help from someone who is not a medical professional.

Save someone's life: Prevent someone from dying by an action you took.

Great lengths: Above and beyond what is necessary.

Do good: Do helpful things for others, animals, the environment, etc.

Do the right thing: Make good choices.

Stay busy: Have lots of things going on.

Free time: Not working or studying.

Break a leg: Wishing someone, "good luck."

Practice

1. Do you want to take a _____ course with me next month?

2. He went to _____ to get into medical school. I'm so happy now that he's a doctor.

3. My philosophy of life is to _____ in this world.

4. Now that I have kids, I don't have any _____.

5. Bob is such a good guy. You can always count on him to _____.

6. Who knows. Maybe you can _____ one day.

7. Hey, _____ tonight. You'll be great!

8. I like to _____ at night so I don't sit on my couch, watch TV, and eat junk food!

Answers

1. first aid

2. great lengths

3. do good

4. free time

5. do the right thing.

6. save someone's life

7. break a leg

8. stay busy

Caught a Cold

Jen and Keith are talking about being sick.

Jen: Oh Keith, you don't look so good!

Keith: I'm **not feeling great**. I **caught a cold** last week.

Jen: Stay away from me! I **can't afford to** get sick. I have a big project coming up.

Keith: No problem! I don't want to be near people. I just had to **pop out** to get some groceries. I'll be back home and spending money **online shopping** to make myself feel better **soon enough**!

Jen: Have some **hot tea** with **lemon and honey**. That always makes me feel better. And make sure to go to the doctor if it starts to get into your chest. I don't want you to catch pneumonia.

Keith: Yes, I will for sure.

Vocabulary

Not feeling great: Feeling under the weather.

Caught a cold: Got sick (sore throat, runny nose, etc.)

Can't afford to: Don't have enough money to do something.

Pop out: Leaving quickly to do something and then coming back.

Online shopping: Buying things using the Internet.

Soon enough: Shortly; in the near future.

Lemon and honey: What some people drink with hot water or tea when they're sick.

Practice

1. I don't think I can come over tonight. I'm _____.

2. I'm pretty sure he _____ from the other kids at school.

3. I much prefer _____ to buying stuff in stores.

4. Sorry, I _____ eat out any more this month! Want to come over instead?

5. I know you miss him but you'll see him _____. Only three more days!

6. I'll _____ and grab some beer. I'll be right back.

7. Why don't you have some hot water with _____? Your throat will feel better.

Answers

1. not feeling great

2. caught a cold

3. online shopping

4. can't afford to

5. soon enough

6. pop out

7. lemon and honey

Talking about Health Problems

Madison and Sara are talking about health problems.

Madison: Hey Sara, how are you doing? I heard that you were in the hospital.

Sara: I was for a few days. I had a weird stomach thing going on. I couldn't keep anything down and I had a very sharp pain in a certain spot. It turned out to be nothing but it was super painful.

Madison: What did the doctors say? They couldn't find anything?

Sara: They did all these tests but nothing came up. They suspected it might be appendicitis. And then it just got better after a few days. It was strange.

Madison: That does sound odd. Well, I'm happy you're feeling better now.

Sara: Me too. It's impossible to sleep in the hospital. I was getting so tired.

Madison: I hope it doesn't happen again.

Check Your Understanding

1. Who was in the hospital?

2. What was wrong with Sara?

3. Why didn't Sara like staying in the hospital?

Answers

1. Sara was in the hospital.

2. She has a painful stomach but the doctors don't know why.

3. She didn't like it because it was difficult to sleep there.

Eating Habits

Sun and Todd are talking about New Year's Resolutions.

Sun: Do you have a **New Year's resolution** planned for 2021?

Todd: A big one! I have high blood pressure so I want to change my **eating habits** by not eating so much **junk food** and **processed food**. I'm going to focus on **home-cooked meals** and smaller **portion sizes**. And less salt too.

Sun: Mine is very similar. My doctor says that my cholesterol is too high. I'm not going to **go on a diet** but I want to eat a **balanced diet** with more **fruits and vegetables**. And I want to avoid the **second helpings**, especially at dinner. That's my **Achilles heel**.

Todd: We should **hold each other accountable**. And what about making plant-based meals and having some potlucks? Maybe once a month?

Sun: Great idea!

Vocabulary

New Year's resolution: Thing you resolve to do for the upcoming year.

Eating habits: General way of eating (can be healthy or unhealthy).

Junk food: Food that isn't healthy. For example, chips and candy.

Processed food: Food that has been manufactured in some way. Often contains lots of sugar, fat and salt.

Home-cooked meals: Food that you cook at home.

Portion sizes: How much food you eat at one time.

Go on a diet: Eat less or differently to try to lose weight.

Balanced diet: A wide variety of healthy foods.

Fruits and vegetables: Fruits and vegetables!

Second helpings: Taking a second portion of a meal after finishing your first portion.

Achilles heel: A weakness in someone who is generally strong.

Hold each other accountable: Check in with each other to help achieve some goal.

Practice

1. Let's _____ for this. I want to get this done under budget.
2. My son eats way too much _____. He probably eats an entire box of crackers a day!
3. I want to _____ so that I can lose weight for my sister's wedding.
4. His _____ is that he procrastinates.
5. Avoid _____ at dinner if you want to drop a few pounds.
6. I love _____ like potato chips and candy.
7. I want to reduce my _____. For example, only one piece of chicken instead of two.
8. It's best to eat a variety of brightly colored _____.
9. My _____ are terrible. I often skip breakfast and then snack late at night.
10. I love my husband's _____.
11. My _____ is to stop smoking.
12. A _____ consists of healthy foods from a variety of food groups.

Answers

1. hold each other accountable
2. processed food
3. go on a diet
4. Achilles heel
5. second helpings
6. junk food
7. portion sizes
8. fruits and vegetables
9. eating habits
10. home-cooked meals
11. New Year's resolution

12. balanced diet

Lifestyle Changes

Kim and Tanya are talking about not feeling well.

Kim: Did you **go to the doctor**? I know you were **not feeling well**.

Tanya: I did. She didn't **diagnose me** with anything but said that I'd need to make some serious **lifestyle changes**. My **overall health** is quite poor. My cholesterol and blood pressure are too high. And my resting heart rate is close to 80.

Kim: Oh no! What did she recommend?

Tanya: She said that I have to **reduce my stress**, **get plenty of sleep**, and **eat a balanced diet**.

Kim: That doesn't sound so bad. Do you have to **quit smoking**?

Tanya: Oh yeah, that too. It **shook me up**. She said that if I didn't change, my **life expectancy** would decrease.

Vocabulary

Go to the doctor: Have an appointment with a doctor.

Not feeling well: Feeling sick.

Diagnose me: Assign a name to a health problem.

Lifestyle changes: Change in what you eat, how much you exercise and other unhealthy habits like smoking or drinking alcohol.

Overall health: General level of healthiness/unhealthiness.

Reduce my stress: Decrease the amount of stress in your life.

Get plenty of sleep: Sleep eight hours a night.

Eat a balanced diet: Eating mostly healthy food from all the food groups.

Quit smoking: Stop using cigarettes.

Shook me up: Made me feel nervous, worried, or anxious.

Life expectancy: How long you can expect to live.

Practice

1. In Canada, the average _____ for men is 84 years.

2. Please _____. It seems like you've been sick for a while now.

3. You'll have to make some _____ to reduce your chance of a heart attack.

4. It _____ when he told me that he wanted to get divorced.

5. I'm _____. I need to go home early today.

6. I hope that I can _____ by changing jobs.

7. My goal is to _____ this year but I know it won't be easy.

8. Please try to _____ if you want to lower your cholesterol.

9. My doctor didn't _____ with anything but just said that I had to stop drinking so much coffee.

10. His _____ is quite good, considering how old he is.

11. Please try to _____ before your exam. You'll be able to think more clearly.

Answers

1. life expectancy

2. go to the doctor

3. lifestyle changes

4. shook me up

5. not feeling well

6. reduce my stress

7. quit smoking

8. eat a balanced diet

9. diagnose me

10. overall health

11. get plenty of sleep

A Terrible Cold

Carrie can't go hiking because she's sick.

Tim: Do you want to go for a quick hike after work today?

Carrie: Oh, I can't. I have a terrible cold.

Tim: Oh no! Did you stay home from work today?

Carrie: Yes. For the past three days. My cough is so bad that I can barely talk or move without coughing. And I had a high fever for the first couple of days.

Tim: Oh friend. That's terrible. Are you getting any better?

Carrie: Yes, today was the first time I got out of bed. I had an online appointment with my doctor too. She said that it's maybe nothing to worry about but I still feel terrible.

Tim: Do you need me to bring you anything?

Carrie: My Mom brought over some homemade soup a couple of days ago. I'm doing okay. And I just got some groceries delivered.

Check your Understanding

1. How long has Carrie been sick?

2. Does Carrie need Tim's help?

3. What did Carrie's Mom bring her?

Answers

1. She's been sick for at least three days.

2. No, she doesn't.

3. She brought her some homemade soup.

Floss your Teeth!

Jenny is talking to Dr. Thomsen about her teeth.

Dr. Thomsen: Hi Jenny, have you had any problems with your teeth?

Jenny: No, I think they're good. No issues.

Dr. Thomsen: How often do you brush and floss?

Jenny: I brush at least twice a day. Always before bed. And flossing...ummm..maybe once a week, if that.

Dr. Thomsen: Okay. That's good for brushing but flossing every day is very important, especially as people get older. You've had a few cavities in the past few years. This is probably why.

Jenny: I know. I'm just so lazy about it.

Dr. Thomsen: Okay, let me have a look and see if there any problems.

Check your Understanding

1. How often does Jenny floss her teeth?

2. How often does she brush her teeth?

3. Does she have any new cavities today?

Answers

1. She flosses once a week or even less than that.

2. She brushes at least twice a day.

3. We're not sure yet.

Talking to the Dental hygienist

Carrie is talking to the dental hygienist.

Dental hygienist: How's your brushing and flossing going?

Carrie: I brush almost every time after I eat. I work from home now so it's easy to do.

Dental hygienist: That's great! That's more than most people.

Dental hygienist: And your flossing?

Carrie: Well, not so great. Maybe once a week but always after I eat something like popcorn.

Dental hygienist: Okay. That's not ideal. You should be doing it every night before bed. It's very easy for food to get stuck between your teeth.

Carrie: I know. I'll do better.

Dental hygienist: Have you tried those flosser things? They're easy to use, even when you're just watching TV or something.

Carrie: No, I haven't. That's a good idea. I'll pick some up next time I'm at the store.

Check your Understanding

1. How often does she brush her teeth?

2. Why should people floss their teeth?

3. What does the dental hygienist recommend to Carrie? Why?

Answers

1. She brushes almost every time after she eats.

2. People should floss because it's easy for food to get stuck in between teeth.

3. She recommends using flossers instead of dental floss because they're easier.

At the Dentist

Sid is talking about her teeth with the dentist.

Dentist: How's your brushing and flossing going? Your x-ray shows two new cavities.

Sid: I brush almost every time after I eat.

Dentist: And your flossing?

Sid: Well, not so great. Maybe once a week.

Dentist: Okay. That's not ideal. You should be doing it every night before bed. It's easy for food to get stuck between teeth and cause cavities.

Sid: I know. I'll do better.

Dentist: Just make it a habit. Do it every day for 30 days and you'll never forget!

Check your Understanding

1. Is Sid good at flossing his teeth?

2. What causes cavities?

3. What does the dentist recommend?

Answers

1. No, he only does it once a week.

2. Food getting stuck between teeth can cause cavities.

3. She recommends flossing every day before bed.

Before You Go

If you found this book useful, please leave a review wherever you bought it. It will help other English learners, like yourself find this resource.

Please send me an email with any questions or feedback that you might have.

YouTube: www.youtube.com/c/jackiebolen

Pinterest: www.pinterest.com/eslspeaking

ESL Speaking: www.eslspeaking.org

Email: jb.business.online@gmail.com

You might also be interested in these books (by Jackie Bolen):

- Short Stories in English for Intermediate Learners

- Master English Collocations in 15 Minutes a Day

- IELTS Academic Vocabulary Builder

ab286bbe-5a23-4a88-806e-486546c64cd0R01